Pulse/Pulso
In Remembrance of Orlando

edited by
Roy G. Guzmán *&* Miguel M. Morales

DAMAGED GOODS PRESS
Richmond, Virginia

Copyright © June 2018 Contributors

Edited by Roy G. Guzmán & Miguel M. Morales
Published by Damaged Goods Press
Publisher Caseyrenée Lopez
www.damagedgoodspress.com

All rights reserved. No part or parts of this book may be reproduced in any format without the expressed written consent of Damaged Goods Press, Roy G. Guzmán, Miguel M. Morales, Caseyrenée Lopez, or individual contributors.

ISBN-13: 978-0-9978267-8-4
ISBN-10: 0-9978267-8-9

Printed in the United States of America
Richmond, Virginia

Cover design and layout by Caseyrenée Lopez

for

Stanley Almodovar III, 23
Amanda L. Alvear, 25
Oscar A. Aracena Montero, 26
Rodolfo Ayala Ayala, 33
Antonio Davon Brown, 29
Darryl Roman Burt II, 29
Angel Candelario-Padro, 28
Juan Chavez Martinez, 25
Luis Daniel Conde, 39
Cory James Connell, 21
Tevin Eugene Crosby, 25
Deonka Deidra Drayton, 32
Simón Adrian Carrillo Fernández, 31
Leroy Valentin Fernandez, 25
Mercedez Marisol Flores, 26
Peter Ommy Gonzalez Cruz, 22
Juan Ramon Guerrero, 22
Paul Terrell Henry, 41
Frank Hernandez, 27
Miguel Angel Honorato, 30
Javier Jorge Reyes, 40
Jason Benjamin Josaphat, 19
Eddie Jamoldroy Justice, 30
Anthony Luis Laureano Disla, 25
Christopher Andrew Leinonen, 32

Alejandro Barrios Martinez, 21
Brenda Marquez McCool, 49
Gilberto R. Silva Menendez, 25
Kimberly Jean Morris, 37
Akyra Monet Murray, 18
Luis Omar Ocasio Capo, 20
Geraldo A. Ortiz Jimenez, 25
Eric Ivan Ortiz-Rivera, 36
Joel Rayon Paniagua, 32
Jean Carlos Mendez Perez, 35
Enrique L. Rios, Jr., 25
Jean Carlos Nieves Rodríguez, 27
Xavier Emmanuel Serrano-Rosado, 35
Christopher Joseph Sanfeliz, 24
Yilmary Rodríguez Solivan, 24
Edward Sotomayor Jr., 34
Shane Evan Tomlinson, 33
Martin Benitez Torres, 33
Jonathan A. Camuy Vega, 24
Juan Pablo Rivera Velázquez, 37
Luis Sergio Vielma, 22
Franky Jimmy DeJesus Velázquez, 50
Luis Daniel Wilson-Leon, 37
Jerald Arthur Wright, 31

contents

foreword

Maya Chinchilla
   Church at Night 9

Baruch Porras-Hernandez
   Ceremonias De La Superviviencia 14

Amal Rana
   The night poetry danced with us 16

Monica Palacios
   We Are Brave 17

James A.H. White
   Stained Glass 18

Nicole Oquendo
   trans- 19
   straight partner of ten years and anyone else 20
   to be born 21

Julia Leslie Guarch
   Shh. Shh. Be Quiet 22

César L. De León
   Safe 24
   Debris 25

June Beshea
   Intruder (Home as A Fallacy) 26

Annette Hope Billings
   Endless 27

j. sebastian alberdi
   in my mother's hometown on the twelfth of june 29

Tessara Dudley
   Mourning Glory 31

Jonathan Moore
   scene 32

Luis Lopez-Maldonado
   Orlando Massacre 33

Joe Jimenez
    If Only My Arms Could Offer Fruit, Let the Sun Be Called— 34
    Some Nights, I Just Want to Hold A Man in My Arms, Because This Would Make Everything Better in My Life— 36

Nathan Alexander Moore
    Angelmaker 37

Caridad Moro-Gronlier
    Pulse: A Memorial in Driftwood, Cannon Beach, OR 39

Chen Chen
    Things the Crows Bring 40

contributors

foreword

The collection of works you now hold is like a rama de olivo extending from first-time, emerging, and established writers. Written in the days and weeks following the shooting at Pulse nightclub on June 12, 2016—which killed 49 and wounded 53 of our own—*Pulse/Pulso: In Remembrance of Orlando* is just one sample of voices seeking to resist a toxic culture of unrestrained gun violence that has extinguished the lives of queer and trans people of color and indigenous peoples.

At the time we gathered these pieces, our physical and emotional wounds were fresh. Unfortunately, two years later, they still are. What drove us to these voices, in particular, was witnessing how the power of a singular voice can lift the spirits of the collective, a collective heavily Latinx, brown, Black, womyn, in love, del barrio, with dreams, and whose hearts must pulsate in each of us, in our histories, in how we tell their stories, and in how we dismantle heteropatriarchy. We left the typical constraints and expectations of MFA workshops away from our selections process, and for that we are proud.

We realize this collection is not enough to dispel the long history of violence, in all its forms, that has intersectionally tried to erase queer and trans people of color and indigenous peoples, but decolonized gestures can go far. At AWP (Association of Writers & Writing Programs) 2017, in Washington D.C., we collaborated on a reading around anthologies honoring the Pulse victims. That same collaboration inspired us to propose a panel for AWP 2018, in Tampa, Florida, just an hour-and-a-half away from the Pulse site. We are aware of the privilege that surrounds conferences such as AWP, and we are committed to bringing this project to places that wouldn't otherwise be accessible to queer and trans people.

The process of finding a publisher for *Pulse/Pulso* was an arduous one, marked unfortunately by elitism, classism, and a blatant disregard for queer and trans people of color and indigenous peoples, especially those coming from nonacademic and working-class backgrounds. The publishing world can be cannibalistic of marginalized writers' suffering. The academic world, too, can be a vicious neocolonialist of creative manifestations, but we remembered the lessons we inherited from our LGBT communities' long histories of civil rights protests, our gritos, our resistencias, and decided to redirect our frustrations and our grief towards creating change. We are fortunate that *Pulse/Pulso* has found a home with Damaged Goods Press, one of the most inclusive spaces for trans and queer writers.

As we move forward, we are inspired by the young queer people of color and indigenous peoples who further our communities' activism by working to prevent further mass shootings and other acts of gun violence. We are grateful to all the writers in this collection and to all the people who shared their time, knowledge, skills, space, and love with us. If any of the poems in this collection move you or those around to imagine a safer world, that is all we can ask.

Always, in solidarity,
Roy G. Guzmán & Miguel M. Morales

Maya Chinchilla
Church at Night

for Orlando

1.

Every time I think of Orlando—I mean
Orrrlaaandoh—with extra Spanish flourish
an ornate word to decorate, to trim, to edge
paintings on a map mark bloody conquest stories

en la Florida a flourish is missing the most colorful of its flowers
so many now without a Pulse

the beat remains while they beat our remains
some for political gain
our thoughts and prayers but nothing else
are with you!

let's play smear the queer so you know what happens
lifeless after a night set aside for the truly living
in your cutest jeans once the worst of your fears:
will I get my life tonight?

2.

not that your death might be your coming out story

or that your last selfie would be used to identify you

by family across borders who loved you and depended on you

because documents even matter in the afterlife

3.

a night out in the open because others
had danced, defied, and rioted

heels and bricks against pigs with night sticks
paddy wagons and little dicks on power trips

getting off on… "Just doing our job to keep the peace"
they fought so that we could feel free

however brief
to get our life, la vida, en el ambiente con la familia

and Pulse mis nenes, chulos, locas hermosos…
when I heard your names I could barely catch my breath:

>The Anthonys, The Frankys, The Jean Carlos, The Amandas, The Martins,
>The Luis-es, The Mercedez, The Marisoles, The Enriques,

brown boys, grown men, girls, and women floating on the gender spectrum,
family and friends hanging out with the children of the night

>The Simons, The Gilbertos, The Javiers,
>The Oscars, The Miguel Angels, The Jorges, The Joels,

mostly twenty-year-olds barely experienced enough to fear anything
proud sissy boys, beefcakes, bears, butches, and fabulous femmes

>The Jasons, The Corys, The Juans, The Shanes, The Ramons,
>The Brendas, The Stanleys, The Rodolfos, The Antonios,

gorditas y flaquitas, puercos, perras, putas y jotas, machas, maripositas

>The Darryls, The Tevins, The Deonkas, The Leroys, The Peters,
>The Pauls, The Franks,The Yilmarys, The Johnathans, The Kimberlys,
>The Edwards, The Geraldos, The Angels,

trans girls, maricones, drag queens, club kids lightning on the dance floor

>The Eddys, The Akyras, The Christophers, The Gerardos, The Erics

schoolgirls, businessmen, loyal husbands, bartenders, djs and go-go dancers
without 401(k)s, pension plans or health care

>Puerto Ricans, Mexicans, Salvadorans, Afro-Latinos

4.

I think of every gay bar
and the rare surviving dyke bars
with their once a month—
or if we're lucky— once a week
"Latin(o) Music Nights!"
the Noche de Queer Cumbias,
las Placitas, the Pan Dulces,
las Escuelitas, the Mangos,
las Botas Locas, the Buttas,

Circus and Arenas, Wet,
Coochielicious, Splashes,
some decorated like a year round
quinceñera
some small like dancing
in someone's living room
Executive Suites, Esta Noche,
Chuparosa, Papi Chulo, the Boss,
Pulse and, and, and—

what was that one for lesbians
that was at the flower market
in San Francisco once a month?
Ah, yes, Canela with those old school
mujeres that have been together
for years
where we made out
in the bathroom that one time
as if we were teenagers
because we never got
to be romantic queer teens.

Do you remember the names
of your first gay bars,
early afternoon tea dances,
house parties and special
POC or Latinx nights?
How we'd meet up to get ready,
a few drinks before entry,
to save our dollars for tacos
to soak up the night life in our belly

5.

With each precious face passing on the screen I am right back in every club
near every small town and big city where I loved and *Liiiiived* and made out
with shy dates and smooth lovers, people who identified one way and maybe later
identified another, that one allegedly straight girl who drank too much and wanted
to dance all up on you, but you promised yourself no more dance floor social work
that could lead to hours of unpaid service, gay boyfriends who would eventually
disappear into the crowd, some of us had codes "don't leave the club without me, girl!
our safe word will be cucumber," others we don't worry about, they'll be back in
a few minutes, or we'll check in tomorrow, the shy ones slowly sipping their beer
in the corner not fully fitting in anywhere, we sang along to all the divas: La India,
Thalia, Selena, Paulina, Gloria, Sonora Dinamita, crushed on gay cowboys with their
pressed slacks, matching boots, belts and hats holding each other tight no matter who

they went home to and the butches and boys who gave me dollars to press tips to the chi chis of every dancing queen.

6.

I'm still not ready to be coherent or make connections
I will never be ready to wake up to this news
I'm trying to keep it moving
I'm not sure why the world keeps spinning
the church bells keep ringing

I want action instead of wishes
don't white wash this story
I need your prayers and thoughts to get more specific
and start asking why

how he over-stayed his visa,
leaving the violence in his country for this?

some families can't get here
mothers and fathers seeking humanitarian permissions
who just want to mourn their babies
erasure revictimizes you

7.

Thought the tears had stopped for now
And then I get that lovely text message from a fellow jota
and I think about our precious lives and our relationship to the night life
where we gossiped and cackled and hungered to be looked at and wanted
and screamed the lyrics to our favorite songs, passed out condoms, flyers for services
then cheered the girls and boys putting on a show

how the boys accidentally, or maybe not so,
would cruise the butcha on my arm

because man, I've been in plenty a straight bar,
that I think are just called bars,
when the bartender friend of your brothers will point and holler
and objectify our kisses
and you will say nothing and I will get rowdy
and tell him to get out of my fucking face

I can't say I was always intentionally queer
that came with a fight, hard won, through shyness and intimidation,
took years after kissing enough femme frogs and butch toads

we were not perfect but at least in the church of la joteria y mariconada
I could pull my date close, that tenderest of queers,

she would giggle that she's too soft to be called butch
and I would say I'll call you whatever pronoun or poetic identifier
just so long as we can make out.

8.

Queerly beloved,
we are gathered here today to get through this thing called life
our story stretched across bloodlines, backrooms and borderlines

We're tired of mourning brown kids, shot by entitled pigs
with guns not meant to stop but destroy

We shouldn't have to carry arms on hips meant for dancing
pretending that makes us safe

We remember, honor, dance through our worst fears.
How do we even find any more tears?

Our job, to keep the beat going,
cause the pulse never stopped,
finding love in hopeless places

We're tired of being so resilient.
Pero, love beats here.[1]

---

[1] "Church at Night" originally appeared in *The Journal for Lesbian and Gay Studies* by Duke University Press

Baruch Porras-Hernandez
Ceremonias De La Superviviencia

at the movies   my eye   on the Exit sign
on the aisles the doorways   the space
between the seat in front of me and my legs
how far could I crawl
before I die?

wednesday   after it happened
I went to a work event at a gay bar   I stood
near the exit when I could when I couldn't
I stood near a window I made sure I could
open and fit through   made sure I could
jump out and land on the roof
of the building next door
just in case
                    after the event
my coworker was leaving
thought about hugging him   but I don't
I waived   asked myself
is this the last time I'm going to see him?

two weeks after the massacre
my partner is getting ready to attend Pride
          I am staying home

I watch him pick out his outfit   I sit
quietly on the couch when he is dressed
he holds me   I hold him a little longer
ask myself
is this the last time I'm going to see him?
he leaves   I feel as if I should go with him
just in case

has I love you   always meant
I would die   holding you
                for people   like us?
has I love you
   always tasted like   two boys
   scared to form the word amor
with their lips   terrified to say things
like   belleza te quiero
                        libertad
     would you   die
         holding me?

when it happens   if it happens
do we run towards the fucker together?
do we die in each other's arms?

I will be your shield
will you be mine?

I've never used my body as a shield
is this what true love is? Is this what queer love is?

If our genes   our DNA
truly hold onto memory
then we remember our ancestor's gay love
remember our ancestor's queer communion
the ceremony of maricones before us
their trauma   their struggle
and if that is in us   then so is their survival!

to all the fuckers out there ready to shoot us down
we will survive you   we have survived fires
     we have survived camps
          we have survived plagues and

     we will survive you

I'm sitting at work   everyone
has moved on to the next tragedy
Nice   Quetta   Baghdad   Istanbul

my eyes focus on the exit sign
then the door   the front lobby
    then back to the exit sign
       the door

the space between my cubicle
and the door

    the exit sign
      the door.

Amal Rana
The night poetry danced with us

Orlando 49
emblazoned on the back of a t-shirt
worn by a white queer
who looked through and past
our table of Latinx, Indigenous, Black, Muslim queers
right in front of her
as if we never existed
as if we were not sitting there
laughing and thriving
radiating life
insistent in our brown, black, mixed skinned existence
as if we were not the brilliance of the sun streaking fire
when it decides to go down on the horizon
as if you were not our queer siblings
familia yaars dildars
our amours our pyars
our everything
shaking beautiful bronzed hips
the night poetry danced with us
before being shot
the night poetry danced with us
before being assumed to be a shooter
the night poetry danced with us
before it became second nature
to check for exits
the night poetry danced with us
before bullets replaced stanzas
before the breath of our beloveds
became a line break
with too much finality
the night poetry danced with us
before we understood
some only value our lives
after we are gone
the night poetry danced with us
until we realized
we were the poem

Monica Palacios
We Are Brave

Somos Orlando siempre y para siempre.

I loved being on stage at the Valencia Rose Cabaret in San Francisco, the first gay comedy club in the nation. I was a 20-something dykeling and this club was a safe space for queer performers. The gentlemen who opened this joint were gay activists and elementary school teachers who set out to create a sanctuary for LGBTQ comedians because the straight comedy clubs circa 1982 were extremely homophobic, racist and sexist. It was common to walk into mainstream clubs and hear white male comics joke about: AIDS, fags, lesbos, bitches--to name a few "hilarious" topics. I never mentioned I was a lesbian on stage at straight clubs because I didn't trust these environments with my life.

But walking into the Valencia Rose was home. The owners, employees, other comics, the audience, all gave me something the straight clubs did not--love, kindness, support and most importantly--community. At this unique space, I could be my whole self; allowing me to feel confident and create one of kind comedy promoting my Chicana lesbian identity. This action was very empowering for me and for other queer Chicanx/Latinx people. I loved when the audience came up to me after shows letting me know they appreciated the positive representation of LGBTQ raza.

Although my family was supportive in their own way, my mom was concerned.
"Why do you have to go on stage and tell people you're gay?" She asked.
"I'm talking about my life like all the other comics…that's all." I replied nonchalantly.
"Ay, what if some hombre wants to hurt you?"

I would kindly laugh off her worry and tell her I could handle the hombres. But in the back of my mind, I always thought: if some nutcase with a gun wanted to live out his homophobia, all he had to do was walk into this club. The only security guard we had--was each other.

We had each other. We have each other. We continue to protect one another from this lucha. The haters can try to take us down with their evil but we're going to love stronger, kiss longer and hold each other tighter. As queer famila, we have been, are, and will always be brave.

James A.H. White
Stained Glass

Fifty—the number of years my mother has lived. The number of paper clips currently interlocked in a small tin bucket on my work desk. According to motivational speaker Gail Blanke, the number of physical and emotional ties you should throw out of your life in order to find it again.

Some say many of them knew each other. It's often like that in our community. It's often like that in a nightclub. We recognize each other. There's no darkness dark enough to interrupt that.

The Orange County Medical Examiner's Office, with assistance from Florida Emergency Mortuary Operations Response System, identified, notified, autopsied (if needed) and released all fifty bodies to next of kin within 72 hours of the incident. That is, all but one victim, whose father wouldn't claim his gay son.

Phonesthesia is the term for sound symbolism, or, relating shapes to sounds. I see shame played like tetherball, see it shaped like the tennis ball as it flies, bound, around that metal pole, hear it on the slap of the child's open hand or deeper-chorused fist. I see shame falling on that victim's burial like the kind of rainstorm written into movie scripts—dark and heavy. I think of it registering unfairly on the faces of the closeted's families when they saw their loved one's body and recognized it as if for the first time.

An installation at Chicago's Contemporary Art Museum featured a row of bodies lined across a gallery and blanketed by white sheets that peaked at the noses and toes hidden but assumed molded beneath. A girl nearby says it all makes her sleepy before she falls to the floor and pretends to sleep—like the dead. On the morning of the shooting, I think of my brothers and sisters inside, not lined but scattered, sleep I imagine made clearer to the young as something much neater, something perhaps much whiter.

I break down hearing about the group that hid in the bathroom but were found then fired on, a couple in a stall injured not only by bullets but shrapnel from the wall and door. Suppose the bathroom stall like a closet. Do you remember huddling? How about holding onto yourself beneath a traditional Jíbarro straw hat or flower bonnet? How did long did you wait before the car horn outside announced it had come to take you out dancing?

Nicole Oquendo
trans-

across beyond and through the point of binding up,
it was easier to tell my mother *me, might be gay*
than to explain the situation: beyond my body:

and therefore no easier to tell her that the pulse
of our collective grieving was me, almost there

no farther from a holy body than the *x*
woven together at the end of *latin*,
because the @ doesn't fit, because i'm neither,
and *might be gay* was easier than the weight of @
binding us together but binding me further in

to be on the other side of man and woman
but on the same side as grieving, wound too tight
to tell her the dead are my family too, that the binder
feels like bullets pressed against my chest

straight partner of ten years and anyone else

do not erase my grief. there is a galaxy of this
spreading out inside my chest. we are at war
and where there is shooting we respond with
grinding and the cupping of a new face. i have
permission to want you and anyone else; there
is no but. we learn as we grow into our bodies,
and society had trained me to mistake heat
for she or between as jealousy or fascination, not love.
i am older now, and know whatever is blossoming
between the legs, with permission, represents ripe
fruit. i can love them and love you too because
there is no them, only us, healing.

to be born

my spine is queer, curved enough
to hold me up while the news bends
and sways us. every day we die, and
one day it will be me, though statistically,
according to these headlines,
it's more likely to happen soon.

but there's new life to look forward to.
last year, my family taught me how
to press into my chest and sculpt my own form.
i make love now by giving and taking in equal measure.
my brothers and sisters and those in between
see me to standing next to them, signing all of my names.

Julia Leslie Guarch
Shh. Shh. Be Quiet

To stay silent is to stay hidden
Under dead bodies of those before us
Who spoke too loudly
Walked too proudly
Who kissed in Miami.

#WeAreOrlando

In the bathrooms we fight to enter,
Our brothers and sisters fought to live:
A refuge from a killer and evidence of hate.
Texts sending last goodbyes and

Im gonna die

A cup passed around to prevent dehydration,
Sipping water and blood.

Mommy I love you

Joshua McGill helps another man,
riddled in gunshot wounds,
limp to safety.
They embrace.

Call the police

The power was off.
It was hot and it reeked of blood.

Call them mommy

Cell phones chirped and rang and chirped and
Were unanswered.

#LoveWins

Hes coming
Im going to die

The first responders called out "If you're alive, raise your hand"
And in a hospital in Massachusetts, I am worrying over my sister-in-law,
Unaware of the news.

My father is watching Peru beat Brazil in soccer
And my mom says, "Oh, did you hear about Orlando?"
As if it's not unusual
As if I should have known.
The normalcy sickens me.

600 calls.

600 calls is too few to express our love.

We can never raise our hands.
We are not alive.
Those bloody bodies were our hearts.
Every gunshot is the music we must face.

Every queer, every latinx has a bullet in their hand
And another in their hip.

The shirt of every sweat and blood drenched sibling
Is our tourniquet.
Every step navigates a splintered floor.

People are stepping over us
While others drag us away,
Limping, crying, staying silent.

"It's still fresh to me," he said.
Our silence stays alive,
And all I hear is *"Shh. Shh. Be Quiet"*

*Whenever I say "I love you"
Whenever I kiss her face.
It always stays the same.*[2]

---

[2] italics are Eddie Jamoldroy Justice's last texts.

César L. De León
Safe

        This

        is where I fly
        boundless
                between
            dashes of light

        songs   on my lips
        songs   on my hips

        I can dazzle
              within the beat
        between
                  our beat

        briefly

        can you see me
        can you   catch me

        can you

        seal the deal
        with a pop   diva
                          kiss

        safe   among
          fearless neon stars

        safe   among
          multitudes of us.

Debris

        i woke up with a butterfly in my throat
        a bee in my ear

                wasn't me

        until i washed
        the debris
        of streetlight nightmares

        off the soles of my feet

        fed the bathtub drain
        swirls of sirens

        like galactic arms.

June Beshea
Intruder (Home as A Fallacy)

The home is a thin glass veil away from being just another grave
a lie given to appease and quiet the night
no, love does not protect us against bullets
all this dance and joy do not protect against destruction
it was all the whispers of how we turned ash to food and fed ourselves
how we died and lived on at the same time that have made us otherworldly
hasn't everyone wanted to push the limits of immortality?
is there not power in knowing what makes the strong weak?
knowing what makes the flesh glitter?
what pumps the heart of the undead?
easy to see why they would want to bloody us-all black and queer and living
a coven in the dark-conjuring hope in b/w the beats of that song we all know.
making life from dust and eating it until our bellies are full with just enough to get by
til there is more of us to be spilled.
and the beat is a myth we made up that night
and the undead are dead again.
someone let themselves into our sanctuary
all they wanted was to know the truth
all they found was disappointment
in how we connected all these bodies in ritual and every wound seems to rip open on us all at once.
how our magic is not a shield but an elixir
meant to stave off what we have always seen coming.

Annette Hope Billings
Endless

Before he left me that night
I stood tiptoe,
drew my beautiful sepia son to me,
enfolded him against my breasts.
He pulled away in mock disapproval
while I planted endless
kisses on his grinning face.
He wiped each place my lips landed,
so in return,
I chose to kiss him all the more.

He responded, "Stop, you'll make me late."
I reminded him mothers should *always*
kiss as if it is their last.

He chuckled, "You'll live to kiss
me until you past one hundred,
until you're abuela—he paused—
"forty-nine times!"

I swatted his bottom as if he was five,
slipped a folded twenty, three condoms
in the pocket of his jeans.
He reached to retrieve my gifts
hooted with laughter at what he found.
I demanded his promise to use them,
he jokes he can always spend more money.

He separates from me to leave,
freezes at the door, comes back
to dance me around the room,
a Miami salsa
I match him step for step.

"Be careful tonight, M'hijo."
"Who me, Mama?" he grinned,
pressed a hand to his heart, said, "Siepre!"

As he walked out into June evening air,
a chill told me someone
had just walked across my grave.

Hours later I startle awake

to his terrified phone call, "Mama!"
then the sound of fireworks?
Voicemail answers my million return calls
"You have reached the man of your dreams
but who I love most is mi madre."

Pulse is so close
I arrived before sirens
to see a lifeless? person laying on the ground,
I screamed to see the son so *still*—
was mine.

I fought EMS, police when they tried
to take him from me
just as I battled delivery
staff after he was born
because I knew no safety more certain
than him circled by my arms.

Before he left me that night
I drew my beautiful sepia son to me,
enfolded him against my breasts
only his warm blood between us
as I planted endless kisses
as if they were my last.[3]

---

[3] "Endless" originally appeared in *Just Shy of Stars*, published by Spartan Press.

j. sebastian alberdi
in my mother's hometown on the twelfth of june

dios no salva, maria.
llenos somos de rabia,
el amor nos maldigo.

//

i never really prayed
ave marias in the morning, si,
when you asked
i would say i had. checking twitter
half-asleep, *there's been another in orlando,*
fifty replaces *buenos días, madre*
and you talk to god.

//

today's breakfast is leche lala, pan dulce,
and from your cousin, details
i didn't tell you — *en un club gay.*

i try to pour myself into my coffee
cinnamoned, but only my eyes
manage to burn.

en serio?

you: past the point of wondering
why i didn't tell you, not past asking
after breakfast
(you love to ask)
why i care so much
that i scare you with how much i care about people;
the 'like them' stinger implied.

//

i'm in mexico with you,
dad too,
all by myself.

//

closing my eyes at church

i see ruby
on a sweat-wet floor;
i try to remember if silence
is a stage of grief
or prayer.

my prayer is about you: *how long
does the first stage last; do i want
to see the second?* i think i feel it
when i'm with you, sometimes anger
after you ask (you love to ask) *porque
te enojas* when you call someone

puto, maricon

words i knew before
queer, before i knew
words for what i was
that didn't burn like mescal
down a gringo throat.

//

there are other poems, wr
all of their poems filled with bursts of love.
i have blood
family that says
that we got what we deserved.
that what happened,
wasn't a hate crime;

where is my lover to reassure me?

//

santa maría, madre de dios,
ruega por nosotros maricones,
ahora y en la hora de nuestra muerte.
amén.

Tessara Dudley
Mourning Glory

The morning after we caught his bullets at the club
they applauded themselves for policing our pride
cis and gay and white they claimed our deaths as their own
wreathed themselves in our tears and pain
rainbow'd our shrouds and claimed we were one

The morning after we caught his bullets at the club
they gathered beside us at the Stonewall Inn
cis and straight and white they spoke false sympathies
stirred us towards hate for hijab and hejazi
hoping forgetfulness for their own legislative sins

The morning after we caught his bullets at the club
"terrorist" flew fast and hot from lips
that never acknowledged their own violence
while newspapers deadnamed Goddess Diamond
denying her dignity even in death

The morning after we caught his bullets at the club
the erasure began to steal away all we own
space proved unsafe for what should have been our freedom
in this world that deems us dark dirty undesirable illegal
we have so very little but this morning is ours alone

Jonathan Jacob Moore
scene

in this scene
i am already gone,
        left sight yesterday
night
in a lyric
or on a body,
my
parents did
not hear me
come home, the
door was silent
with old grief.
i am
pixels and
press release,
got stuck
in a closet
and couldn't find the keyhole in time.

                                            the list
                                          is harder
                                    to pronounce
                                      than most
                                but easier than
                                    Nagasaki.

our freedom, nuclear.
i thought a warm
drink had spilled and
it was radiation, a
shot and two
and three hundred
more
warm kisses later
here I am, still
being
buried
under the mayhem's music.

Luis Lopez-Maldonado
Orlando Massacre

for gay clubs everywhere

They say the violent assault of color & music exploded like popcorn, how horror bloomed on black & brown faces, how a chorus of rainbow screams screeched & pleaded.

They say he was on Grindr hours before sending smiley faces galore, how the world began to mourn after he signed off, 50 mothers' wombs shrinking & shrieking with fear: I re-bun my *chonogo mariconero* & light a cigarette, cheap wine in my right & somewhere behind my skin a queer brown boi weeps, thinking:

God, how can my brothers & sisters fall fall fall like bombs, hit dancefloor & spread like glitter, frozen eyes color splashed on walls?

Joe Jimenez
If Only My Arms Could Offer Fruit, Let the Sun Be Called—

If only my arms could offer
fruit, let the sun be called—

my petition against memory is
to quit drinking autobiography
                              as
if it were seedless—

but sometimes a memory is a
hard habit to kick:

one inkling of last year's bouts,
& all night, sadness clotting its
dark cloth

over each eye, over the mouth,
all its clout—.

Perhaps you need only to have
loved a man & lost him
                            to
see this.

But when a man, dying, opens
the mouth the whole world
tells us does not exist: we
appreciate offers
to think of no one,

that silence of letting the body
be only its body—
                      which is a
challenge when all your life
you have eaten silence.

Huge gobs. Slices of asteroids,
slivers & spoonfuls of moon.
Bouts of bobbing

not for apples, not for air or
fisticuffs, the head going
down,

coming up,

because, on its account, the
head is really just
the body & was born
& deserves to use the mouth

for other tasks besides talking,
besides chewing.
                Yes, the
body has more choices
than it knows—.
                Yes, I have
witnessed other men's arms
bear fruit— .

But perhaps I am wrong, & no
one has to have lost his heart
to understand this:

the most beautiful thing I have
ever seen was a man taking a
jar

of his lover's dark ash &
throwing him
over fence slats, through them,
onto the green lawn, toward
the White House,

& yelling his name, yelling it &
yelling it.
At that point, I only wanted
                          to
know my body, which means
to have it be known,

which means to feel myself in
another man's blood, or

to hear myself called even
when I'm gone—.[4]

---

[4] "If Only My Arms Could Offer Fruit, Let the Sun Be Called—" originally appeared in *Bat City Review*.

Some Nights, I Just Want to Hold A Man in My Arms, Because This Would Make Everything Better in My Life—

a comfort I frame—biceps and all
of my Mexican tattoos, my chest and my stuttering lung,
the whispers that only come from another man's eyes
when the whole world inside him is a fingernail
or quiet like a small bucket of snails.
Even when I'm pissed, and rage fills my throat like a brume,
moreso, then, especially, I wish my kiss tenderness,
enough to make a man's heart burst
into a thousand desert owls—the wingbeat,
the featherness, the beak prod, the swarm-crouch and screech—.
Last week, I was a pendulum in a fantasy—versatile,
swinging back, forth, into, deeply.
Being entered is when I know I am human.
Being entered is when I know I'm a part of something bigger.
Again. Equilibrium—.
Evenness—. And here it is: I've come here to love
the breath in my bones when skin falls off the world.
and Who doesn't carry some sort of skein on his knuckles?
The moment inside the body
when joy is not born as much as it is made out of anything
the rest of the world doesn't want.

Nathan Alexander Moore
Angelmaker

> *for my siblings in Orlando & elsewhere*

1

I hear the dirge of sirens and the hiss of contention
This is how I know it could have been me
Another night Another club Another drink away
From my world tilting, fluttering into permanent darkness
To be given wings I never asked for

2

He has glittered the other me with bullets
I watched the silver screen ticker with the bodies of my siblings
They were still sweating blood
He has anointed them with crooked, twisted iron
But this time it wasn't a cross
Afterwards, we all danced the terrifying skitter and stumble
Of the morning after

3

We are a family that is used to sharing wounds
It's a part of our inheritance
But we heal together, in the dark
In alcoves of shadow and sin, night clubs become cathedrals
Divine transgressions
We say our benedictions, take communion & community with each other
Amen, A woman, A beautiful strange unspeakable thing
Over our sacrament of shots, we give each other a self that is wholly unholy and clean
Our debauchery is a righteous revelry
This is the closest thing
We can find to an earthly paradise
But there are still snakes in the garden
And we are reminded again
Of whom Adam should rightfully be with

4

I bet
His scales were sacred
And as cold as a minister's retribution
I bet

His fangs were many and piercing
103 at least, of that I can be sure
I bet
His coils were as long as centuries upon centuries of bloated Scripture,
His flesh like scrolls upon scrolls upon scrolls of Leviticus muscle memory
Constricting, unflinching
I bet
He started small though
Like the shriveled serpent sheathed in many a man's thighs
We must have taunted, tempted, teased or terrified him
Is that why he bit and tore and swallowed?
Is that why he decided to made angels out of fairies?
I bet
He didn't know that his kith of crusaders
are the ones that force us into solitude

5

Our temple was ravaged
Last night
the smoke of our incenses were scattered to the four winds,
mixing with screams and sorrow
Our prayers were interrupted, shattered
Broken into shards within the bloody thunder of air
Our sacred saintly sisters, dolled up in their most beautiful vestments
Were pushed out of the grotto
Our holy mothers
Reduced to rumble
Our sacrosanct shadows are not sanctioned
So we are reminded today

To build the altar again
We come together again
We cry over these crimes,
baptizing our bloody belabored bodies
We cleave together in the cloisters again
Again
Again
A-gain
Wretchedly hallowed
This is the closest thing we have to worship
This is the nearest we come to redeemed

Caridad Moro-Gronlier
Pulse: A Memorial in Driftwood, Cannon Beach, OR

I have crossed a continent
to cast forty-nine names into the sea
cuarenta y nueve nombres mangled
by anchors—Flores, Paniagua, Sanfeliz—
on a beach strewn with bones
of giants: Redwood, Sequoia, Sitka Spruce.
Behemoths that would not stay buried.

Before the ruined beauty of this necropolis
saplings cleaved to elders, grew
stronger in each other's arms
as they danced in darkened groves,
lit by the strobe of sunlight, dappled
limbs akimbo, unprepared for annihilation,
unprepared for the spilled sap, the glint
of the axe, the buzz saw, the prayers
planted at the root of their destruction.

I step over titans battered down
to driftwood, stripped of tannin and pulp,
bark bleached white as sheets and offer
forty-nine names to the sea
cuarenta y nueve nombres al mar.

Here I can believe the ocean
returns what she is given.[5]

---

[5] "Pulse: A Memorial in Driftwood, Cannon Beach, OR" originally appeared in *SWWIM Every Day*.

Chen Chen
Things the Crows Bring

An eggy disaster. An opulently abandoned theatre. A jade box of childhood
fears. A downtown renewal. A wedding vow renewal. A library book overdue
& despised. A highway beautification with a rerun of the full moon. An infomercial
they would really like us to watch, in formalwear. Their aunts who each bring just

a thimble of thunder. Their grandmothers who bring us geodes to crack:
a jack, a jenny. Twins! The crows bring us ancient selfies they took
with baby Jesus. Overpriced dental plans. Adulthood. Fondue & dipping breads
but we're already full. Other birds but we don't care about them. Words we've

spoken to our parents that we would take back. That we wouldn't.
The blue pen that exploded. The Oneida County Welcome Center. What bees
wear at night when they want to feel sexy. The math of Halley's comet. A miracle
but we just couldn't accept, no no, that's far too much, you're too kind, no.

Jasmine tea. Income tax. Property tax. War but they see our hands
are already full of it. So. The notion that if we mourned every single person
killed just today. Learned the name & wept the name.
If we had the body. To grieve every body.

They bring it to our doorstep.

Editors

Roy G. Guzmán was born in Honduras and is currently pursuing a PhD in Cultural Studies and Comparative Literature at the University of Minnesota. Roy is a 2017 Ruth Lilly and Dorothy Sargent Rosenberg Poetry Fellow. Roy's debut collection will be published by Graywolf Press. Visit Roy online at roygguzman.com.

Miguel M. Morales grew up in Texas working as a migrant/seasonal farmworker. He is a Lambda Literary Fellow and an alum of the Macondo Writers Workshop. He is a member of the Latino Writers Collective, a founding member of Brown Voices/Brown Pulse and of La Resistencia. His work appears in *From Macho to Mariposa: New Gay Latino Fiction*, *Imaniman: Poets Writing in the Anzaldúan Borderlands*, *Primera Página: Poetry from the Latino Heartland*, *Duende Journal*, *Acentos Review*, *Green Mountains Review*, *Texas Poetry Review*, and *The Hawai'i Review*, among others. He is also the co-editor of a forthcoming anthology centering the voices of Kansas City's Queer Latinx familia.

Contributors

Maya Chinchilla, author of *The Cha Cha Files: A Chapina Poética*, is a queer femme Guatemalan writer and educator. She gives readings, lectures, writing workshops, and also teaches as a lecturer at UC Davis, UC Santa Cruz, and San Francisco State University in creative writing and Latino/a/x Studies. She is the editor of the forthcoming *CentroMariconadas*, an anthology of queer and trans Central American writing. Find out more about Maya at mayachapina.com.

Baruch Porras-Hernandez is a writer and performer based in San Francisco. His work appears in *Drunk in a Midnight Choir*, *The Tusk*, *Foglifter*, *Divining Divas* (Lethe Press), *Assaracus* (Sibling Rivalry Press), and Write Bloody Publishing. He is a Lambda Literary Fellow in Poetry and Playwriting, and is the head organizer for ¿Donde Esta Mi Gente?, a Latinx Literary Series.

Amal Rana is a queer Pakistani Poet and Muslim futurist. Her work has appeared in multiple anthologies and literary journals. In a time when even exhaling while being Muslim is perceived as a crime, Amal conjures poetry as an invocation for collective liberation.

Monica Palacios is the creator of solo performances, plays, screenplays, short stories, poems, essays, featuring the Latinx LGBTQ experience. National and international scholars have critically engaged her work in academic journals, books, dissertations and conference panels. Monica is the Lucille Geier Lakes Writer-in-Residence at Smith College, Spring 2019. Find Monica online at www.monicapalacios.com.

James A.H. White is a gay, first-generation U.S. immigrant. His writing appears or is forthcoming in *Best New British & Irish Poets 2018*, *Black Warrior Review*, *Colorado Review*, *Lambda Literary*, and *Washington Square Review*, among others. Author of *hiku [pull]* (Porkbelly Press), James recently relocated from South Florida to Maryland. Follow James on Twitter @jamesahwhite.

Nicole Oquendo has appeared in the chapbooks *some prophets*, *self is wolf*, *wringing gendered we*, and *Space Baby*, and the hybrid memoir *Telomeres*. She is currently serving as an Assistant Editor for Sundress Publications and is the editor of the forthcoming anthology *Manticore: Hybrid Writing from Hybrid Identities*.

Julia Leslie Guarch is not friends with pronouns. She hates them all equally, so he doesn't care which you use. Julia is a social justice artist who happens to be a queer poet. Their poems appear in *Triadæ Magazine*, *Impossible Archetype*, *Fearsome Critters Art Magazine*, *Sunset Liminal*, and elsewhere. She was a finalist for the Iceland Writers Retreat Alumni Award, the MacKnight Black Poetry Award, and received special mention in the Jean Corrie Poetry Contest. Julia was recently elected as the VP for the LGBTQ Writers Caucus.

César L. De León is a poet-organizer for Resistencia: Poets Against Walls and a member of the Chocholichex writing collective. His work has appeared in *Pilgrimage*, *The Acentos Review*, *La Bloga*, and the anthologies *Imaniman: Poets Writing in the Anzaldúan Borderlands* (Aunt Lute, 2016) and *Texas Weather* (Lamar University, 2016), among others.

June Beshea is a queer poet from Atlanta, GA. They are a member of House DaLorde an Afro femme centered queer house based out of wherever they end up.

Annette Hope Billings is an award-winning poet and actress. Her work has been published in a variety of print and online publications. Her most recent poetry collection is *Just Shy of Stars* (Spartan Press, 2018).

j. sebastián alberdi writes plays & poems about being queer, mexican, and brought up in his mother's catholicism. he runs *pnkprl*, an erasure e-zine, and is a lambda literary fellow. his first book of erasures *YES* is available from ghost city press.

Tessara Dudley is a historian-in-training and a poet making art at the intersection of Jewish working-class Black queer femme disabled life. Her hobbies include studying Torah, fighting oppression, building safer communities, and knitting. Tessara can be found at tessaradudley.com.

Jonathan Jacob Moore is Black and vengeful. His work has appeared in *Drome Magazine*, *The James Franco Review*, *RaceBaitR*, *Vinyl*, and elsewhere. He is Book Reviewer at *The Shade Journal*, Fellowship Director at *Winter Tangerine*, and a Ph.D. student in the Department of African American Studies at UC Berkeley.

Luis Lopez-Maldonado is a Xicanx poeta, playwright, dancer, choreographer, and educator. He earned a Bachelor of Arts degree from the University of California Riverside in Creative Writing and Dance. His poetry has appeared in *The American Poetry Review*, *Foglifter*, *The Packinghouse Review*, *Public Pool*, and *Spillway*, among many others. He also earned a Master of Arts degree in Dance from Florida State University, and a Master of Fine Arts degree in Creative Writing from the University of Notre Dame. He is currently a co-founder and editor at *The Brillantina Project*. Find Luis at luislopez-maldonado.com.

Joe Jiménez is the author of *The Possibilities of Mud* (Korima, 2014) and *Bloodline* (Arte Público, 2016). Jiménez's next collection *Rattlesnake Allegory* (Red Hen, 2019) is forthcoming. His essays and poems have recently appeared in *The Adroit Journal*, *Iron Horse*, *RHINO*, *Aster(ix)*, and *Waxwing*, and on the PBS NewsHour and Lambda Literary sites. Jimenez was awarded a Lucas Artists Literary Artists Fellowship from 2017-2020. He lives in San Antonio, Texas, and is a member of the Macondo Writing Workshops. For more information, visit joejimenez.net.

Nathan Alexander Moore is a genderfluid writer, scholar, and dreamer. He is interested in critical and creative methods to explore the nuances of blackness, queerness, memory, history, identity, and trauma. He recently graduated from SUNY Buffalo with an MA in Innovative Writing and is currently working on his first novel.

Caridad Moro-Gronlier is the author of *Visionware* (Finishing Line Press). The recipient of an Elizabeth George Foundation Grant and a Florida Artist Fellowship, her work has appeared in *Reading Queer*, *The Notre Dame Review*, *The Lavender*, and others. She resides in Miami, FL with her wife and son.

Chen Chen is the author of *When I Grow Up I Want to Be a List of Further Possibilities*, which won the Thom Gunn Award for Gay Poetry and was longlisted for a National Book Award, among other honors. Chen is the 2018-2020 Jacob Ziskind Poet-in-Residence at Brandeis University.

Made in the USA
Columbia, SC
07 August 2018